ORACLES FOR
NIGHT-BLOOMING ECCENTRICS

Poems by Nancy Berg

BLUE LIGHT PRESS ◆ 1ST WORLD PUBLISHING

1st WORLD
PUBLISHING

SAN FRANCISCO ◆ FAIRFIELD ◆ DELHI

Winner of the 2009 Blue Light Book Award
ORACLES FOR NIGHT-BLOOMING ECCENTRICS
Copyright ©2009 by Nancy Berg

BLUE LIGHT PRESS
1563 45th Avenue
San Francisco, California, 94122

1ST WORLD PUBLISHING
641-209-5000

AUTHOR
nancyberg.com
nancyberg@earthlink.net

BOOK DESIGN
Melanie Gendron

COVER & INTERIOR ART
Melanie Gendron
melaniegendron.com

PHOTOGRAPH
Robert Sabaroff

FIRST EDITION

LCCN: 2009923487

ISBN: 978-1-59540-906-5

What People are Saying About

ORACLES FOR NIGHT-BLOOMING ECCENTRICS

"Right out of the headlines, participant in, on and of the edges of the dangerous and 'bejeweled' world, listener of sages ubiquitous, public radio opinionated, cable tv hysterical, spinning on the deck of the luxury liner of night itself with an 'Excedrin habit' and a penchant for small dogs and oracular insomnia, this is Nancy Berg's poetry, seeking its soulmate inside an emerald and unlike anything else being written, 'crackling like early electricity,' heavy with art. When will this walking full-production Hollywood musical of a poet come to your town and make you a deal deep inside, 'tangling all arteries' with her abundant literary grace and charm? You can only hope and dream. But she is here now in this booty-kicking little number. So, pick it up, try it on. It looks great on you."

— Rustin Larson, author of *Crazy Star* and *Islands*

"If Kafka is accurate in his assertion that a book should serve as an ax for the frozen sea within us, and I believe he is, then Nancy Berg's poems accomplish this exact task by a gentler, and nurturing alchemy. *Oracles for Night-Blooming Eccentrics* holds us to its breast, rocking us, whispering its lullabies of disappoint, hope, and creation, urging us to warm. I came to it chilled by the world and was thawed by the heat of its plangent and triumphant honesty. Such is the power of Berg's truly fine poems."

—Mark Spragg, author of *An Unfinished Life, The Fruit of Stone,* and *Where Rivers Change Direction*

"You don't have to be eccentric—night-blooming or otherwise—to savor Nancy Berg's enchanting vision. It helps, though, to want to see as eccentrics see, with unfiltered eyes and deconditioned minds and hearts as open as canyons to sublime, mysterious delights dressed up as ordinary. This is poetry as revelation."

— Phil Goldberg, author of *This is Next Year, Roadsigns* and *The Intuitive Edge*

"Not easy, one would imagine, to write a volume on the intersection between longing, being in the moment, metaphysics, and love as a unifying theory of consciousness. Perhaps more difficult to do so with such sensitivity and wry humor. Nancy's done more than that in her poems, beautifully centered in such humanity, weaving entire stories into single poems that also display life lessons. . . Her poems are beautiful, mesmerizing, and instructive — they communicate so much about passion for life and beauty, for living with longing for the eternity of the moment and for finding that moment with clarity, insight, passion, and joy, that I feel more alive having read them. Can't think of a better place to begin to practice some conscious living and detachment than by reading Nancy Berg's *Oracles for Night-Blooming Eccentrics*."

    — Steven D'Ambrose, Writers' Guild of America

"Upon first reading, Nancy Berg's poetry affected me greatly. Upon repeated readings over the following months, it mapped out a different way of thinking about the world that is generous without limit and deep beyond measure. And upon reading Berg's manuscript so many times that it has become a dog-eared, overly-post-it-noted mess on my bookshelf, it has become clear to me that it is the very best book that I have read throughout my forties, with images that come to mind almost daily and a point of view that suffuses my life, giving me a way to live the ideals I deeply believe in."

    —David Groves, Executive Director of Freedom to Read, L.A., Past President of American Society of Journalists and Authors, Los Angeles

"This stuff is good. Poetry for the 21st Century. Honest. Poignant. Filled with hope, desire, wit, charm, and beauty. To read Nancy Berg is to come face to face, eyeball to eyeball with the contemporary human condition. . . yet find yourself wanting more. To read Nancy Berg is to be filled with awe and sometimes even envy. I feel like this! I laugh and cry like this! Why can't I *write* like this? To read Nancy Berg is to discover a soulmate who, in singing what it's like to be herself, embraces what it's like to be you. And me. All of us. *All the way.*"

    — Larry Brody, award-winning writer/producer, Director of Cloud Creek Institute for the Arts

"*Oracles for Night Blooming Eccentrics* are poems of a generous spirit. Nancy Berg is a master of characterization, with poems inhabited by journeys to the miraculous, painful, and gritty places where the soul lives. Her poems 'burn a hole in your palm' or make love on islands ripped by a hurricane. Always edgy and beatific, 'perching in dangerous places like a sparrow on a high voltage wire,' they speak the language of dolphins. They sing in the language of the soul."

— Diane Frank, author of *Entering the Word Temple* and *Blackberries in the Dream House*

"Real poets praise life. Not that they don't see the darkness and feel the pain. But they know it's part of an all-embracing Whole in which, as Nancy Berg tells us, "everything above and below the unclouded sky/feels surprisingly worthy of love." In her unique and authentic voice, Berg invites us to share that vision. This is delicious poetry, filled with memorable lines, aha insights, laughter, tears, and, yes, beauty. Like all significant art, it gets better each time you return to it."

— Jack Forem, co-author of *What the Bleep Do We Know!?* and *Awakening the Leader Within*

"Nancy Berg, a visionary poet excavating the depths of human experience, has created a shattering and hilarious chronicle of our planet and our time."

— Dan Carbone, Playwright, Bay Area Theatre Critics Circle Award-winner

"Nancy Berg's poems do such complete justice to the craziness of the world, and to the author's own, that I have to believe every small and delicate affirmation. . . . More than that, I can't help smiling with delight that all this rich craziness IS. And even more than that, these poems make me want to be as crazy as I am. . . Thus, it is clear, these poems have the power to inspire at least temporary enlightenment—and to make one realize just how dangerous that is."

— Silvine Farnell, Ph.D., Host, *Voices of Silence* radio program, creator of "Deeper Into Poetry" workshops

" . . . My favorite artists make me laugh and cry. Charlie Chaplin all at once. So does Nancy Berg . . . Nancy's poems overwhelm me with an experience that cannot be refuted: 'Life is worth living.' "

—Michael Berry, Playwright, humorist, author of *The Drummer's Bible*

IN LOVING MEMORY OF BOB SABAROFF

"Three things in human life are important:
The first is to be kind.
The second is to be kind.
The third is to be kind."

—Henry James

"Let us be kinder to one another."

—last words of Aldous Huxley

Contents

I

SINGING HYMNS

AND

BARKING

I Could Have Danced All Night If I Hadn't Spontaneously Combusted

When it was still there in August,
my landlady threatened to call the fire department.
The pine needles were already so thick and dry
and sharp on the carpet,
even with socks on,
you couldn't walk without drawing blood.
But I was in love
and it was bigger than anything they'd ever shown on television.
My Christmas tree had become a Magnificent Obsession.
It was more than the red, black, fuschia, and turquoise lace
draped around it,
or the *Rudraksha*, crystal, and angelskin coral.
It was more than the gracefully curved plastic corkscrew drinking straw
and the brass pennywhistle all the way from Ireland
balanced skillfully in the nether branches.
It was more than the paper boats made of theatre programs
or the ecumenical touches—
luminous postcards of St. Anne and the Virgin,
Krishna neatly shellacked on a maple leaf,
the copper ornament that spelled *Shalom* in English and Hebrew.
It was more than every piece of cheap, miraculous jewelry
I ever used to turn *myself* into a Christmas tree.
It was more than the fact that they never let me have one
when I was a kid
because I was Jewish.
It was more even than the most spectacular neon star
you ever saw
wearing a long striped hawk feather
at exactly the same jaunty angle
Maurice Chevalier wore his perfect straw hat.
(The package said
"DO NOT MAKE THIS STAR STEADY BURNING"
but I did it anyway and burnt out all the miniature bulbs,

wanting, as always, too much at once.)
But God, it was more than all that.

There was something that made me keep that tree
through Valentine's Day
and hang little pastel hearts all over it.
There was something, on Easter,
that made me hang all those hollow eggs
I decorated myself
with Day-Glo paint
and macaroni.
I had to stop letting people over—they didn't understand.
My Christmas tree and I celebrated the Fourth of July together.
I wore a red, white, and blue jumpsuit.
The tree wore at least 100 tiny American flags.

You see, when they said my Christmas tree had become
a fire hazard,
I knew they didn't mean somebody would strike a match nearby.
It was a fire hazard
because someday it would spontaneously combust
from the intense heat of its own unbearable beauty.
And I was waiting,
ready to see at least one of us go out
in a supremely self-sufficient blaze of glory.

It was right there on page 433 in the Book of Lists
between the brain radiation levels of 60 celebrated persons
and a collection of 10 people who had Stigmata.
There it was in glorious black and white:
"Eight Cases of Spontaneous Combustion."
And while I realized I might never develop holy wounds
on my hands and feet,
and the only person who knew how to measure brain radiation
died in 1952,
deep inside I knew that some day,
with the flawless timing of a fine Swiss watch,
I had as good a chance as anybody to spontaneously combust.

Just like Euphemia Johnson, age 68,
who spontaneously blazed one rainy day in England
while drinking her afternoon tea.

Or Mr. and Mrs. Patrick Rooney
who crossed over together one Christmas Eve
during the second chorus of "Silent Night"
when Mrs. Rooney suddenly turned into a pillar of fire
and Mr. Rooney died from the smoke in the air.
That one went deep.
Now I know when people say
"Do you love me?"
they really mean:
"If I spontaneously combusted, would you inhale the smoke?"

But best by far,
Miss Phyllis Newcombe,
age 22,
who probably spent 3 or 4 months
perfecting a pink organdy gown
with pearl buttons, a polka dot sash,
and baby blue lace at the collar and cuffs,
just to wear to the dance hall that night on August 7th
when she waltzed with the prettiest man there—
the one with the strongest arms
and the wisest eyes
and the prettiest white teeth.
The music was like satin and velvet;
like those luscious chocolate caramels
she once got for Valentine's Day.
She was so radiant everyone was staring;
even the people waltzing kept craning their necks to look at her.
Something was becoming more and more curiously alive
about the room.
It seemed the air itself was waltzing
1-2-3. . . 1-2-3. . . 1-2-3. . . 1-2-3. . .
It must have been on a 2

that Miss Newcombe smiled exquisitely
and happily burst into flames.

Neither Miss Newcombe's partner
nor the pink organdy gown
were as much as singed.
For a split second the gown hovered in mid-air,
as if confused.
Then, with nothing left to cover,
it dropped delicately to the floor
like a rose petal.

I like to imagine Miss Newcombe's partner understood.
That he picked up the dress
and quietly left the hall
while everyone else went crazy.

People and Christmas trees who spontaneously combust
go to a secret place
where everything is switched on and awake.
Those little golden particles
you see when you're excited
are constantly vibrating in the air.

Miss Newcombe *had* to combust.
She'd never be 22 again
in that gown
on that night
with that man
with those teeth.
Here, she moves in a state of constant consummation
with the dazzling uniqueness of an albino giraffe.
All the trees are Christmas trees
with silver garlands and sequins
and those electric glass ornaments
with bubbling water.
Every moment is always, always, always enough.

SMALLEST DOG IN THE WORLD

for Billie

Seeking a soulmate, I bought a dog afraid of everything.
Hunched shoulders,
morbid shivering,
upper back pliable as a slab of oak;
people were always asking us if we were cold.

"That animal is almost too sensitive for life,"
says a friend.
I nod, blushing,
possibly even twitching,
stooping to paw at the stress-related hives on my leg.

I blanketed that dog
with a love so thick
it was far too gelatinous and rich
for any human.
Cooing incessantly,
I hovered, enveloped,
and watched her uncurl.
Now she bares her teeth at pit bulls
and flirts shamelessly with strangers.
So this is how you make a creature strong,
I see,
somewhat later than most
and yet still in this lifetime.

"Doctor—help!
I can't stop singing to my dog."
"What could be more natural?," says the doctor.
"The heart yearns to praise."

"Doctor—help!
I can't stop kissing my dog
on the forehead."

"How could it be otherwise?," says the doctor.
"The heart yearns for beauty."

The smallest dog in the world
shares my penchant for fanaticism.
There we are, in the L.A. paper,
under "Poet Spreads the Word About Red Cross."
That's me in the beret, like some terrorist of mercy;
the sacred chihuahua's wrapped head to claw
in the international symbol for neutrality.
(I'm surprised I don't have Red Cross nipple piercings
and little Clara Barton-shaped decals on each tooth.)

"Doctor—help!
Hearing that 'Dog' is 'God' spelled backwards,
I have once again confused my priorities."
"Absolutely normal," says the doctor.
"The heart yearns for imaginary significance."
(Or did he say,
"The heart yearns for solace?")

The smallest dog in the world
scares away macho dudes
and emotional diabetics
who lack the blood sugar
for progressively saccharine terms of endearment.
This, I suspect, is a blessing.
That noise you hear is the pager,
the phone, the fax, and the door,
all of which we seem to be ignoring as usual.
Wrapped in fetal position
around the smallest dog in the world,
I have learned to form the perfect circle.

"Doctor—help!
I can't stop thinking about my dog:
when I'm out on a date,
when a man comes close,

when. . ."
"Impeccable choice," says the doctor,
waving snapshots of his beagle.
"A dog will give you more love in an hour
than a spouse can offer in a hundred years."

The smallest dog in the world is more than
a mere fashion accessory.
There I am in velvet
at an elegant formal affair.
"I didn't recognize you without your other half,"
sneers a socialite.
At this the boundaries of selfhood evaporate,
as if they have attempted to pay by check
without a driver's license.

"Doctor—help!
I can't stop babytalking my dog."
"It's about time" says the doctor,
sounding suspiciously like my mother.
"Biology is destiny."

PEACE OUT

Yes,
I am the woman
who flipped the bird
at the guys in the tricked out Mustang
who almost ran me over
as I walked to the peace vigil,
and yes,
I was wearing
a perfectly round
white on black
replica vintage
peace button
at the time,
though no,
I am not entirely without
a sense
of the basic laws
of microcosm/macrocosm
metaphysics,
but listen,
those guys looked like
they aimed the car
directly at me
on purpose,
and hey
as I'm sure you've noticed,
you can take the girl
out of New York but. . .
You're right.
I am holding a sign
that clearly indicates
I don't want
anyone's
18 year old kid

dropping bombs
on skinny families
in my name,
so yes,
I might try to be
a little more like
the gentle-eyed,
candle-holding activist
chanting next to me
at the vigil.
That's right,
the one who smiled
when somebody
reached a hand through
the sunroof
of a silver Nissan
to give us the finger. . .
the one who said,
"Oh look!
Half a peace sign.
He must be an amputee."

ORACLES FOR NIGHT-BLOOMING ECCENTRICS

for Bob, who is now luxuriating in his bright Good Night

Stand here, alert, topdeck
on this bejeweled ship,
darkness all brilliant about you
like Joseph's coat,
and tell me it is wrong to be nocturnal.

Oracles are everywhere.
Yes, we hate to admit
that after decades of guilt-inflamed daylight phobia,
we finally came to understand ourselves
through the copy in a Pinot Grigio commercial.
"Evening falls," it says,
"The world softens a bit
about the edges."
Of course.
How obvious.
It's sharp edges we've been avoiding all our lives—
a measured course for an emotional hemophiliac—
and really not a character flaw after all.

So now we see ourselves as some
trembling, diaphanous
smoke ring of a person,
afraid to open our eyes
until dim light turns
the menacing corners of things
into comfortingly vague and indistinct smudges.
Jarred, we reconstruct that vision:
our emotions may be fragile,
but our spirit is a 350 pound
female trucker in a buzz cut
with a huge tattoo on her proud left buttock.
It reads:
"Hallelujah. You got a problem with that?"

The trouble is, oracles are everywhere.
On National Public Radio they mention
that even the oldest, simplest,
doughnut-shaped bacteria
came complete with circadian rhythms.
These single-celled characters
could sense when dawn and dusk approached,
and *they* never failed to respond appropriately.
The commentator strangely forgets his crisp reserve,
regressing to a previous incarnation
as an AM shock jock.
"Let me get this straight," he quips,
"we're talking about pond scum
that gets jet lag."

OK, we got it.
People like us are less functional than pond scum,
and although we've long intuited such a truth,
it hurts, nonetheless,
to hear it spelled out in words.
Like that wretched Ambien ad
they run ever so cynically
with "Buffy, the Vampire Slayer."
"There's a rhythm to life," it says.
"We sleep at night
and wake in the morning."
And then the evil sponsors abbreviate time
to show us this gorgeous,
promiscuous flower—
it unfurls its sweet petals
triumphantly,
seductively,
to engorge its hot lover the sun.

No, our petals
will not open for just any
ostentatious body of light.

So what if we need to be
coaxed into consciousness
by the ice-blue riff
of the Gibbous moon
or licked awake
by the moist, cleansing sheen
of a Geminid Shower?
If you'd seen that poster in the ladies' room
of your local health food store,
you'd know that blossoms
come in all degrees of delicacy,
and if an artichoke can be classified
as a flower,
then, damn it,
so can we.

Alright, then,
we're night-blooming jasmine,
and it makes perfect sense
that we didn't find our own twin consort
until five minutes before
we had to run a classified like
"Exotic, nocturnal, perimenopausal woman
with CNN and Excedrin habit
seeks luminous, enabling
creature of the night
for extreme unction
for extreme solicitude."

It makes sense that we had to meet him
well past the witching hour,
at a coffeehouse
featuring post-impressionist photographs
of the Fetish Ball;
a coffeehouse peddling do-it-yourself voodoo kits
and handcuffs covered with fake pink fur;
a place splashed everywhere with its own blazing slogan:
"Death Before Decaf."

Yes, stand alert, topdeck, on this bejeweled ship,
darkness all brilliant about you
like Joseph's coat,
silence so lush and endless
you'll rise inside it,
pulsing
and powerful,
87% pure and
100% organic. . .
You're green-limbed,
expansive
and all-forgiving
as any vegan vampire
anywhere.

Summer lightning
streams out of the top of your skull
with such innocent velocity. . .

Is that a snake in your spine
or are you just happy to be
awake when nobody else is?

How the Star Got Inside the Trapiche Emerald

Raw music was her gift
Beauty like the ache of language
A green twice as true
as all grassland swirls
stretched among sea
on her cloud-draped planet
He swore to make her the eye of God
Ezekiel's wheel
queen of the night in this arc of space

She says: I a stone and you a star
He says: I a glint and you a focus
She says: Stars so rarely enter us

She is stillness;
he wrenches a hole in the sky
Here this crystalline iris, open
Here the blaze as he falls to his life

CAT'S EYE EMERALD:
THE GEOMETRY OF DESIRE

Now that the want cook
has you stalking
holy mist
on a green mountain lake;
now that you haven't slept
once all summer,
trailing one streamer
of restless
light;
now that you orbit
a cat's eye emerald,
sweeping through sacraments,
weak-limbed with love;
know that this radiance
never will leave you—
once you are blessed
you are blessed to the bone.

DOLPHIN REPORT

Look inside the center of my heart.
You'll find a newspaper clipping of yourself
in your white First Communion veil
or a snapshot of your grandson at his Bar Mitzvah,
smiling in front of the chopped liver swan.
I am in love from the moment I am born
until the moment I die.
Why else would I leap thirty feet in the air,
whistling and clicking,
spinning seven times
before I touch down in the dark sea
where I am born, tail-first
and nudged to the surface to breathe;
before I even taste the rich milk of my mother
I fall in love with everything above and below sea level.
With the currents pressing fast on my soft, new skin,
with the sun sending shafts through the top of the ocean,
with the woman on the boat in the yellow scarf
shouting, pointing,
holding a drink and a camera in one hand.
When I am in love I swim like a fish,
fly like a bird,
and breathe like a man.

Listen to the center of my heart.
You'll hear that quiet song you used to sing over and over
in a thin, high voice
when your mother thought you were asleep.
The awkward, tinny piano of your first recital.
You'll hear the joke about the sailor
that will still make you laugh
five minutes before
you close your eyes for the last time in this body.

It patterns my face in a fixed grin
and lets me glide and play on the waves from your ships,
falling backward
into joy crackling like early electricity.
But that same love
makes me need to guide those ships
every night for twenty years
through the sharp coral reefs of Australia.
The same love that lets me hold you to the surface
when you're drowning
makes me cling to an abandoned dinghy
like a giant rag doll.
It makes me haunt one beach for ten years
waiting for a dead boy to ride on my back.
That which lifts me up also weighs me down,
but you already understand this.
I live only to breathe in unison.

So I learn to speak without vocal chords
and recognize geometric shapes in waterproof books.
Small things like this make you so happy.
But look inside the center of my heart.
You'll find a hologram
of the part of you you've been wanting to worship
for a long, long time.

COCOONING

You're fine, really,
but the small burrowing creature inside you
is trying to live in a hot cubbyhole
six and a half feet beneath the foundation
of your co-op.
Everything's OK, you guess,
except this burrowing animal
keeps trying to claw its way inside
the wombs of your lovers
who are men
and, as such, without wombs
but the burrowing creature refuses to understand this.
Your life, it hisses, has been breathing into the microphone
for longer than you can remember,
and a tableaux series of your most embarrassing moments
is painted in primary colors
on a caravan of 18-wheelers,
coming soon to a neighborhood near you.
"Feed me three or four down comforters,"
says the burrower.
"Feed me nine electric blankets.
Let me hang my cubist paintings,
all in earth tones,
on the wall."
Over time, it will contract you
to a dense black dot
beneath the shadow of your navel.
It will fold you in a closet
intermittently pumped with oxygen
by convoluted theories on a conspiracy of mule deer
and the nature of the spirit to betray, consume, and spit.

Your impulse will be to surrender,
but your mission will be to resist.

Desperately Seeking Stigmata

Like Edvard Munch, my landscape is heavy with premonition.
Having dreamt all night about John the Baptist,
I wake up rasping out the opening to *Godspell*.
This terrifies the dog,
who feels once again accosted by light—
she's a fieldmouse hidden in a Monet wheatstack.
"No more MGM screenings for you, my love,
and no more epiphany-stalking missions to the Getty."
We are desperately seeking Stigmata
(or some tidier sign of Annunciation).

Ophthalmology

Today, my eye doctor tells me
I am overcompensating in all areas of life.
If anything ever comes closer than
sixteen inches away from my face
I must pretend not to see it.
What you can't see can't hurt you,
my eye doctor says, with his hand on my leg,
he says life is just a spy novel anyway, or should be.
Still, they warned about women like me in medical school—
how we must never be kissed with our eyes open;
how a lover's gaze closer than sixteen inches away
would scramble the already confused community
of our ill-coordinated muscles and those
prematurely aging optic nerves.
How our fears of emotional intimacy
are grounded in visual danger.
"Your right eye has not been introduced to your left,"
my eye doctor says.
"You only imagine that you are imagining your nausea.
The obvious root is your sympathetic nervous system—
both erratically wired and decidedly lacking in sympathy."
Still, I am grateful he does not ask me
to decipher a single chart.
He discusses instead the wonders of moral complexity,
how, as he sees it,
Winston Churchill's personal assassin was conceived
for the good of us all;
and this in contrast to the ethical void
of that bomb in Lord Mountbatten's motorboat—
the man who never had to pay for drinks
and probably had a lot to live for.
Before I leave, my eye doctor prescribes
an extra prism for each lens
so I will not be burdened with unnecessary unity,

so all that is whole will be separated at once
into red, orange, and yellow.
The green, blue, indigo, and violet are for my next visit,
my eye doctor says.
As the glasses get thicker
the world will take on tones cool as water;
all objects held at a comfortable distance
will appear, at least,
to have innocent intentions.

LET'S MAKE A DEAL

I have a crisp, new fifty dollar bill
for any member of the studio audience
who can reach the deepest scar inside her heart
with the tip of her tongue.

One hundred dollars
for anyone in a turquoise rooster suit
who can let the pain behind that scar
crackle full force
through every network of nerves in her body,
frying all circuits
tangling all arteries
scraping each cell
like a jagged-edged blade.

I've got an all expenses paid trip to Bermuda
for anyone with pale peach lipstick in her purse
who can throw her head all the way back
and guzzle the emptiness behind that pain
like Lite beer
like nectar
like that sacred high school love potion:
pink lemonade and vodka.

I'm offering every consumable prize
behind every Door Number Two
that ever was
every cherry red Corvette convertible
every glistening dinette set
every entertainment console
fairly bursting with
state-of-the-nanosecond music system
and God's own oversized Plasma TV
to anyone who can sit alive and awake

in the middle of that emptiness
until it fills up
with the sight, scent, and breath
of a wildflower forest
until her spirit stretches
slow and voluptuous
as the laziest note from a low-wailing sax
until everything above and below the unclouded sky
feels surprisingly worthy of love.

The Vandalization of Sweet Mercy

I am not usually a woman
who names her car six weeks before she buys it
who names it Sweet Mercy
in honor of every
turbo-charged spiral of forgiveness
that touches us
quickly,
lightly,
on top of our heads,
whispering that somehow
we're allowed to be happy
if only for a moment
if only until the next
irrevocable mistake
which will also be forgiven
which will carry in its arms
the promise
of another bright spiral
and eventually another.

Forgive me.
Something has happened to my biological clock.
When other women close their eyes
and see pink and white babies,
I close my eyes
and see little red sports cars
Zero to 130 miles per hour
in point-two-five seconds.
When other people are slowing down
to inch their way over railroad tracks,
I am for some reason
speeding up,
gathering momentum
to take those tracks
in one magnificent flying leap.

There is little time to unravel complexities,
why
on the 33rd morning
of my 33rd year
I awoke with the hormones of a 16 year old boy,
why, when I heard that God's own agile chariot
had been in a wreck
and would be fixed
and would be almost affordable
it took me six months to convince myself
I deserved such a spiral.
Six months of carrying
its photo in my briefcase;
six months of wondering
if someone would slit my throat
or slash my tires
or straighten my hair
if I owned such a car,
and finally,
when I brought Sweet Mercy home
that Friday afternoon
and it was too late
for the birds to sing their morningsong
and too early
for the birds to sing their eveningsong
they were singing anyway,
the closest thing to an *Aria*
that had ever come out of their beaks.

He makes an appearance in my dreams sometimes;
the owner of the pellet gun does.
He says, "I am the red thread
quietly sewn into each of your garments
while your thoughts are busy elsewhere;
I am the crooked, discolored tooth
in the smile of your beloved;
the flaw that keeps you from drowning
in a sea of free-floating anxiety."

And so I understand
it was an act of the deepest possible love
when he relieved me
of the awful burden
of Sweet Mercy's complete perfection
by shooting that bullet hole
right in the middle of her windshield
right in the middle of the night
less than five days after I bought her.

The cracks spread out like a glorious sunburst
like the intricate pattern in the web of a spider
jagged circles
and intersecting lines
with a uniqueness
only a snowflake would understand.

And then there was this sense of holy calm.
Sweet Mercy with a pellet gun hole
was a car I could feel comfortable in.
And while I was still fairly sure
Sweet Mercy would find some way to abandon me,
the bond between us grew even deeper.
On Libertyville Road
at 100 miles an hour
this car like a funnel
blowing prayers into my brain.

The change creeps in silently,
gradually.
We are waiting at stoplights
and that feeling of contact with the road is going,
slowly.
Sweet Mercy,
who was never born for gravity,
is beginning to lose all patience with pretending.
I fill her up with every kind of ballast I can find:

bags of rock salt,
hard-bound anthologies,
heavy, if minor, household appliances,
but trunk space was never Sweet Mercy's forte
and we run out of room for ballast
in less than the space of a heartbeat.

The chant creeps in
behind my eyes
behind my ears
I knew you would leave me
I knew I didn't deserve you;
but Sweet Mercy has no time to listen to this.
She is trying to tell me
we are going back home to the Pleiades,
that I am going with her,
we are joined at the hip—
she has no power to go anywhere without me.

There is no time to pack
and less room for luggage,
only a note to leave.
Forgive me
it says
I almost completed
my Amnesty International membership form
lost in the jungle of paperwork under my desk.
Forgive me
I was almost ready
to write four letters a week
to political prisoners
in Central America
and the Persian Gulf but
Forgive me
I am a very good girl but a little disorganized.

Forgive me
it says
I have never been very good at forgiving
Somebody always has to come along
to help pry open my small white fingers
to help me let go
of the saddest color of memory
the kind that burns a hole
in your palm
the kind that burns a hole
in your heart.

But Sweet Mercy has no patience for this.
She thinks the guilt we carry
like halters around our necks
is the most extravagant form
of earthly self-indulgence.
She says
this is what keeps the rains from coming on time
this is why people go hungry.
She begins to rise,
floating away with me
before I have finished the last forgive me.
My words trail off in a scrawl across the page.
We are lifting high above
anything that tastes like
anything but hope,
anything less symmetrical
than the matching handles of the Big and Little Dipper.
Sweet Mercy
who no longer needs a radar detector
exceeded the speed of light
about a thousand planets ago.
Still, the sky before us is not looking back,
the sky is breathing ever so quietly.

II

APARTMENTS
IN THE
AFTERLIFE

COLUMBIA

We should have known by their faces
when they floated on TV—
they had fallen irrevocably in love
with weightlessness.
Blue shirts above,
red shirts below,
they tangled arms and hovered,
a formation reminiscent
of the painted sacred heart.
Had 300-proof elation
ever been so undiluted
among real grownups?

Four virgins,
three second-timers—
these were seven grateful astronauts
who could hardly believe their luck.
The closest they had come to this rapture
had never been terribly close:
Kalpana from the Punjab
chasing rivers in her small plane,
the Navy flight surgeon spinning, flipping,
that unlikely year before med school
when he briefly dazzled crowds in a circus.
But here, as operatic sunset
filled the overhead flight deck windows,
each could see their own reflection,
and superimposed on one's own mirrored pupil,
the bright and dark sides of the earth, in whole,
with all the endless sky around it.

Red sprites and blue tendrils
awaken the fringes of night;
electrical cousins of lightning
flashing up instead of down.

Roses smell different in space,
yet travel quite easily from bud to bloom.
Silkworms hatch into moths,
puffing out redundant wings.
Without earth's magnetic field,
flames are no longer shaped like teardrops.
The crew sets tiny bouncing fireballs,
dousing them easily with simple fog.
Huge clouds of dust arise and disperse
far, far above the west coast of Africa.
Willie McCool smoothly levitates
to capture a flying spoon with his mouth.
And the crystalline blue marble
finely mottled white with clouds
looks so gentle without borders,
the Aurora Australis
spraying earthshine at the moon.

After 16 days they'd found their space legs,
and who among us could bear to relinquish this?
Who among us could bear to return
where every thought is set in stone?
Strapped tight in orange pressure suits,
the seven as one divested themselves
of their last remaining burden of gravity.

Just four days before the blazing,
Florida Today ran this headline:
"Columbia's Astronauts Find Small Miracles
of Life and Light."
Small miracles, we've heard,
can be especially addictive.
The first one may be free,
but soon you crave bigger and bigger miracles,
signs and wonders all around you.
A vault of light is wide and deep,
and the Helix Nebula, we understand,
is anything but overrated.

APARTMENTS IN THE AFTERLIFE

It pains us to think
the apolitical may have an advantage there.
Faith without works is dead, we thought.
They never tried to free the blameless
suck poison out of drinking water
pry guns from the hands of 8 year olds.
On the other hand,
unlike us,
they never visualized
politicians
chopped finely in a Cuisinart
or fed slowly through a wood chipper;
they never pictured heads of state
osterized into nutritious summer drinks
in a 16-speed Motorola smoothie-making machine.
There comes a time when we have to face it—
if thoughts are things,
if words solidify into form
on any plane at all,
we haven't exactly earned
a Malibu-style beach house
in the Afterlife.
Consider the apolitical.
They never worked
to prevent this obscenity of war
indelible
disfiguring
a Karposi's Sarcoma on the face of history,
but they *can* watch the 11 o'clock news
without shrieking obscenity-laden threats
involving hatchets
or similar instruments of mayhem.
They may yet smile their way
into celestial hillside villas

with panoramic floor to ceiling views
of the City of Light.
As for us,
with our violent ravings.
we might reasonably shoot for
a one-bedroom walk-up,
but it's wise, as we know,
to avoid expectations,
and there's much to be said
for the compact ease
of the efficiency apartment.
(One rarely has to call an exterminator
in the Afterlife.)
And no,
those 9,637 peanut butter sandwiches
we zealously proffered to the hungry and houseless
will not have been forgotten.
We will,
like everyone else,
have access to all the Common Areas.
Heaven, we've been told,
has a mixed economy,
studded with blessedly egalitarian elements.
The scat-singing roses,
for example,
are thrilled almost to the point of ignition
to enchant one and all
with their perfumed,
miraculously layered harmonies.
And the Mother of all Light Shows,
with its ultimate synesthesia
its colors so welcoming
its patterns so effusive, so impossibly exhilarating—
yes, the Mother of all Light shows
is absolutely free
for absolutely everyone.
In our present grounded state, we can comfort ourselves
with patter:

"When the Rapture comes, can I have your car?
Your Hummer? Your jet ski?
Your profusion of shoes?"
We can remember
that even the puniest apartment in the Afterlife
will certainly be less cluttered
than any place we've ever lived on earth.
And who needs a built-in waterfall Jacuzzi
when we can just step outside
and be instantly coated with Grace?
Same as those people who never
got worked up enough
about world events
to imagine dismembering
the titular powers that be.
The difference is,
we ranters will not show up
with the permanently pinched foreheads
of the endlessly repressed.
We ranters,
tension-free,
will finally close our eyes
and hear the roses sing.

Swing Low, Sweet Pontiac

for the late, great Roger Kaputnik

My father said there's a tollbooth
on the way to the Sweet Hereafter
and I have to say I'm strangely honored
that in at least one Vicodin vision
he chose to be carried to infinity
in my red 17-year-old Pontiac Sunbird
with its dirty white *schmata*-top
three hubcaps
and the continual high-pitched squeal
of a drill at a discount dentist.
This is one sunbird that never learned to fly,
I want to tell him;
it crawls from zero to 25
in a little more than an hour and a half.
But my father's in no rush, I guess,
and I'm thinking if good intentions
can be converted to currency *anywhere*,
it surely must be there,
at that dazzling tollbooth.
In this case the currency's all in the bumper stickers:
"Practice Random Kindness and Senseless Acts of Beauty"
on its field of purple
directly above the license plate;
"Wage Peace" scrawled in white letters on aquamarine;
"Save Tibet" on that flag of twin snow lions
and fierce geometry of light;
and over to the left, the tender, if prosaic,
"A Home for Every Animal Begins with a Place in the Heart."
I'm glad I never found the anti-nuclear classic
that said *"The Meek Don't Want It"*
beside a drawing of the earth,
since this might have offended the character in the tollbooth.

While it's true that here, in this temporal realm,
my earnest bumper stickers
at best provide reading material
for the rare bored driver not texting
or applying mascara,
I think my father tried to see them
as proof that his sad-eyed daughter
turned out to be a relatively magnanimous person after all.
Mistaking my mother for me,
he asks if we will be taking the top down for this journey,
and I'm thinking,
if not now, when?
The heavenly cartoonist and I
can inch our way to timelessness
with the wind in whatever hair we have left,
singing "Beauty is Truth; Truth, Beauty,"
preparing to trade all we needed to know on earth
for all we need to know hereafter.

Neptune Society Afternoon

You would mostly remember the flowers,
how when the captain handed them out,
everyone held them differently,
some in pockets
some fanned out across laps
some carried stiffly at arm's length,
as if those people never had flowers in their hands before.
They were chrysanthemums and bachelor buttons
and forget-me-nots,
most likely,
all yellow and white, amber and rose.
You could tell some guests were disappointed
they were only allowed to throw flowers in the water,
instead of ashes,
but the captain knew the wind by heart,
and she'd seen too many squeamish mourners
powdered with facefuls of blown back human remains.
You'd remember how the ashes and the flowers
mixed together on the ocean,
how the ashes billowed out like the holy ghost
(in a surprisingly human shape),
how you're pretty sure you heard your father beside you,
laughing:
"They actually think that's
me *down there!*
Can you **believe** *it?"*
You'd remember how someone said we'd scattered his ashes
in the same spot
where a depth charge sank a Japanese submarine
fully loaded down with motorcycles
for spies to use in America,
and how your father, the veteran of Iwo Jima,
would probably like that.
You'd certainly remember how the first mate said

his own father had been in a concentration camp,
how he'd only heard that man laugh twice in his life,
once when he was reading a cartoon *your* father wrote.
How happy the first mate was
that he'd scattered his own father's ashes
right here in approximately the same place.
You'd remember the air was warm and the sea was calm,
and how all the flowers stayed together,
how you could still see them clustered, embracing that spot
as the boat chugged back toward San Pedro Harbor.

Chinese Ghost Wedding

"A few of the guests allow as how, yes, one might think that marrying dead people is bizarre. But as an occasional feature of life in these parts for longer than anyone can remember, ghost marriages are just another relic of ancient China."

—Michael Kramer, TIME Magazine

You could say they wouldn't have loved each other
in the flesh,
she being obsessed,
somehow,
with the inner life of Margaret Thatcher,
he being obsessed
with the same jet black Yamaha 650
that found its final home
halfway embedded in a wall
in a village not far from Beijing.
Now five days later
the new refrigerator and color TV
go to the bride's parents.
The groom's family,
once again in the wrong place at the wrong time,
walk away with only a lecture—
some state-sponsored cremation man
angry about wasting precious land
on bodies instead of crops.
But then of course there's the reassurance
of a son
and a daughter
so sated with connubial bliss
they have little time
or inclination
for uninvited appearances
in kitchens
or even in dreams.
And of course, when the two were alive,
you could say

there were too many questions,
everybody asking Who, What, When, Where, How
and especially *Why* do you love,
as if the mind could embrace such shadows,
as if the half-formed currents of the heart
could stand any more confusion.
How when the cancer took her,
she thought she was being taken by a lover,
her last inhale touched,
somehow,
by the breath
of peach blossoms
and the quiet singularity of death itself.
You could say she
melted off waiting,
unaware of her brothers and sisters
kneeling awkwardly
by the door;
just as you could say he roared off growling,
thinking only of the twisted chrome
and wasted fuel,
but in both cases
you could just as easily be wrong as right.
There's how the two families together
lost four nieces
and two nephews
in Tiananman Square,
with very little to show for it. . .
Still, the point is,
it may have taken only three dollars
to exhume the bride,
but they waited five months
for the right opportunity.
All the thickness of factory air
swept away by the latest typhoon;
the last transistor radio
placed carefully inside the double grave—
there was never a prettier day for a wedding.

THE MYSTERIOUS CASE OF THE SPECTACULAR CADAVER

Gail, in death, was six times more beautiful
than most women achieve at the peak of their bloom.
Of course she was—as we all will be—
but I make no attempt here to speak about Spirit.
It was the abandoned vehicle,
the inevitably sallow shell:
missing all its teeth from a 30-year-old taxi collision,
wasted to the usual near-skeletal mass,
yet lending, mysteriously,
empirically speaking,
a new definition to the term "drop dead gorgeous."
Why would we consider closing her eyes—
those heavy-lidded,
almond-shaped
Kama Sutra illustrations
that rushed young men's blood to unexpected places
when she took her 56-year-old self for a stroll.
Now, fixed on the infinite,
they were yet more compelling.
What more could we add?
We scattered random rose petals
and searched the apartment
for spiritual icons.
We found the Virgin of Guadalupe
in the mouth of a spoon
and a defiantly exultant and scarified
blue clay nude pagan goddess.
On her right we placed
rosewood Quan Yin
by glittering Lakshmi pillow. . .
we were happy to realize
only much later
that not one of the deities present
was male.

No one else dared,
but I found, in a drawer,
an impressively raspberry-chocolate hued lipstick
and tinted her mouth as I knew she would like.
There was much to attend to
in other rooms,
but we each snuck back in
to stare,
to admire.
Firmly rooted in this century,
we were all too embarrassed
to ask the obvious question:
"Do you think it would be really, really weird
to take a picture?"
I eventually spoke up,
to a roar of agreement,
and the camera clicked, flashing
again and again.
Of course, by then
some time had passed
and the initial, miraculous perfection was fading;
yet I remain convinced
this was not the sole reason
why later, at home,
when my photographs arrived,
that dazzling beauty was all but impossible to detect.
Every cliché has to spring up from someplace—
"I guess you had to be there"
is apparently no exception.
I, for one,
am grateful to have been there.
I, for one,
will never be the same.

A Blessing on Your Head, Hand, and Foot

Grandma and Grandpa
get lost at Ellis Island.
All those long lines of people who smell like
sausage,
or stale beer,
or 67 days on a boat,
or anything outside of a *shtetl* in Lithuania. . .
It must be very confusing.

Somehow,
instead of Brooklyn,
they wind up in New Rochelle,
where everybody else is
Irish,
or Italian,
or Black,
where the whole place is founded by
French people, the Huguenots,
who leave France because they want to pray to
Somebody unpopular,
or maybe because they want to pray to
Somebody popular
in an unpopular way.

So Grandpa's tune
Hanteleh. . . fooseleh. . .
sounds French inside my head,
as if the Huguenots leave behind
something in the air
that makes any song the
Irish,
or Italians,
or Blacks,
or one Jewish family sing
sound vaguely like *"Sur La Pont D'Avignon."*

Grandpa opens the Queen City Delicatessen
on Main Street in New Rochelle.
He gets the Irish,
and Italians,
and Blacks,
and even a few Republicans
to develop a taste for *kreplach* soup,
and stuffed *derma,*
and *kugel,*
and somehow,
(perhaps another legacy of the Huguenots),
the fattest french fries anyone has ever seen.

Grandma and Grandpa
don't leave Lithuania because they want to pray to
Somebody unpopular
or even pray to
Somebody popular
in an unpopular way.
They are widely considered to have made a poor choice
in the way they are born.
Grandma stops praying when she is twelve,
about halfway through
one of the more exciting midnight *pogroms.*
It isn't when they are tying various parts of Uncle Abe
to various horses,
but later,
when they get the horses to gallop in various directions.
Her faith goes away
all at once,
like a virgin's pink flower.
She waits and waits,
but it never grows back.

Still, for some reason,
she keeps kosher all her life.
She feeds me *mandelbrod*
you would never believe was baked by an atheist,

and when she takes down the combs,
she lets me sit on her lap
and brush the longest white hair in the world.

shayneh punam, shayneh keppeleh, shayneh velt
beautiful face, beautiful head, beautiful world

Next I sit on Grandpa's lap and we do the song.
Hanteleh. . . fooseleh. . .
He puts down the Yiddish newspaper
and points out my hands, my feet.
Outside the window,
old men sit on benches
with or without grey fedoras,
but mostly with.
Across the street
eleven sparrows
perch on the branch of a tree.

Grandma and Grandpa are my mother's parents.
My father imagines they have somehow hurt him,
and will not allow them in our tiny apartment.
New York is filled with aunts and uncles and
grandparents and cousins
on both sides
who are not allowed in our tiny apartment.
There is no room for them anyway.

They all come to me in my sleep,
in their functional family units.
They are like "Father Knows Best"
or "The Donna Reed Show,"
only these are Mediterranean people,
so they're more visibly affectionate.
I try both code words to get in the circle—
hanteleh. . . fooseleh—
but they are not interested in body parts,
and certainly not extremities.

Grandma has a stroke,
and she finishes her life
in an ecumenical nursing home.
When Grandpa dies,
My mother sits *shivah* for ten days.
Her tears make the first
permanent lines beneath her eyes.
When the time for sitting on wood has past,
My mother still refuses
to sit on roughly half the chairs
in the apartment.
Later, when she and my father move to California
and buy all new chairs,
she refuses to sit on most of them, too.
I take my hands, my feet,
to the Midwest,
where almost nobody has ever tasted *matzo brei*,
and nothing sounds French except Grandpa's Yiddish song.
I keep a *mezzuzeh* on my door,
but from time to time
I also light a candle to the Virgin.

My prayers bounce off the walls
in a garbled hybrid
of every language
in which I've ever learned
even one mispronounced word.
Still,
once in a great while,
I can swear I see
a blessing,
a *broucha*,
filter out through the window screen
and perch on the branch of a tree.

ON THE TRAIL OF X

I thought I was dumber than a pile of bricks.
The identity of X was a singularly unattainable concept,
dark and mysterious as the chain-smoking bad boys
at Davenport Beach.
My algebra teacher was a skinny man with
no indigenous love of numbers
and a face twice as pale as my own myopic perception
of the cold December moon.
His name, by some sublime coincidence, was Mr. Whitehead.
The world had been so unkind to Mr. Whitehead
that he drew in all his senses,
leaving one slender trickle of nasal monologue behind,
designed specifically to lull eighth graders
into hypnogogic states.
One mention of co-equivalents
and my mind went out bargain-hunting for acorns
with the lone black squirrel in Hudson Park.
I was failing algebra,
and you don't fail tuition-paying students
at New Rochelle Academy.
Mr. Whitehead and I were going down together.

Enter the math major cousin,
engaged, if necessary, to surgically implant
algebraic equations into my brain.
He was taking a break from the ever-present smell of curry,
from the six-legged silverfish
he called the state animal of New York,
from his own take-your-life-in-your hands taxi driving
in the Bronx.
They called him Angel Eddy
and he had this core none of us could touch.
There was a light in his eye forever trained
on some unique diffraction of visible radio waves

bouncing off a snow-covered peak in the Andes
or maybe the Alps.
The math major cousin thought everything was funny,
and he made me think everything was funny.
He was the kindest presence I had ever known.

Some things don't change.
We open the algebra book on this white formica table
and my mind flies away to some wispy pink realm
where I'm dancing the frug with Davy Jones
to the acid bubblegum beat of the latest Monkees song.
Three number-crammed pages go by and I don't even notice.
The light in the eyes of the math major cousin
reshapes itself
into this amused "Aha!" experience and he says
"You're not stupid—
you just find this stuff so incredibly boring
you can't pay attention."
There is no particular light in my eye,
but I manage to have my own "Aha!" experience.
Yes, I think,
this is probably true about
a whole bunch of things
I find impossible.
It's not like some insipid song about confidence
from a 50s movie.
Instead it's real.
And some of it actually sticks.

Yes, I passed algebra.
No, I never trained my mind to perch in dangerous places
like a sparrow on a high voltage wire.
Mr. Whitehead basically kicked me upstairs
to rescue the prep school from stigma.
And a few years later the math major cousin
was master of ceremonies in his hospital bed,
healing the Philippina nurses with an audacious love
and calming down the rest of us with a peace so thick

we would mold it into furniture and sit on it.
We said he had the most beautiful bone structure in America.

There are people you say you would die for,
but this is more feasibly said than done.
It works OK when your loved ones fall off bridges
or get trapped in burning buildings,
but when they're betrayed inside
by the composition of their own blood,
you can't do much more than be a bearer of balloons
and tire them out by talking.
Still, this is *our* grief.
The math major cousin fought that cancer
like some life-crazed nationalist for ten years.
Then one day he said, "This pain is unacceptable,"
blessed the water he was given to drink, making it holy,
and let his soul float out like a nomadic hybrid
of eagle and dove.
Once again on the trail of X,
it spiraled with a graceful ferocity around the room.

On the day of Eddy's funeral,
his horoscope emphasized spiritual dimensions
and the finding of lost love.
It said *"You are finally free from an obligation
it was foolish to take on in the first place."*
Spot on, I think, holding up the weight
of my own solid body,
placing the unrevealed alias of X
in a hollow air pocket
smack in the middle of my chest.
This as a time capsule
for unexpected excavations
on the other side.
This, at some point, as an offering
to the first radiant algebra tutor I meet.

III

WHERE EVERYTHING IS SWITCHED ON AND AWAKE

DEFYING THE MYSTERY RASH

new in town

It must be somehow genetic,
this fear of land and people
instead of ocean and animal;
my uncle, but for Hitler,
was to swim in the Berlin Olympics.
We are a small club,
those of us who trust our bodies to this toxic water:
Central Americans, accustomed to lifelong danger,
hybrid children, with their heightened awareness
of the winds
that blow through all of us,
and I, stalking a grace and buoyancy
I never dared fantasize on unfriendly earth.
Even the homeless won't risk the mystery rash—
they refuse to immerse themselves anywhere south of Malibu.
Still, swimming out past the pelicans and turning to shore,
L.A. looks like a gentle, airbrushed resort.
One imagines it's actually peacetime.
On dry land,
I fear this city, burning, haunted,
turning its hollow core back on itself;
I fear the small sounds of my ground floor apartment;
I'm afraid to park my car in my own locked garage
without a steering club, blinking alarm, and ignition kill switch.
In water, I see no reason to come back.
Trying to remember those cues from childhood—
You get out when your lips turn purple;
You get out when the palms of your hands
pucker and wrinkle,
pickled in brine like a umeboshi plum.
You get out when your skin
begins to imitate
the skin of a featherless bird,
goose bumps. . . chicken skin. . .

You get out, they say, when you're water-logged.
But what exactly does water-logged mean?
Surfers developing flu-like symptoms
and overnight conversions to ecology,
gangbangers too young to drive their mothers' cars
assassinating each other on the cool, dark sand...
Still, I say, this is where poems live.
Lapped by the undertow I bark like a dog;
rocked by the deep,
my spirit stretches three or four times further
than the arc of my personal fears.
I saw a stingray captured in Santa Monica Bay.
He sailed through the air on that taut white line,
waving his rare, flat wings,
opening and closing his mouth on the crowded pier.
A boy cut off his stinger, for some reason,
and threw him back.
And yes, we go from one body of water to another,
sea creatures, captured,
waiting to drown in the storm-tossed bodily fluids
of the phantom lover,
waiting to follow that languid trickle of light
where the sun or the moon hits the water,
waiting to get drunk and drunk out of our minds
on a beauty we may never live to taste.
Strangely, for now, this is almost enough.
I will cling to this baptism,
pathogenic and luminous.
I am
singing hymns and barking
in the filthy, magnificent sea.

KAUA'I

with gratitude for excerpts from the Kumulipo, an ancient
Hawaiian creation chant

Iniki, they say, was a torrent of flowers
This piercing wind gone heavy with frangipani
ragged breath on fire with torch ginger and red hibiscus,
a harsh whip woven from deep purple orchids
and white plumeria.
You can't defoliate a garden island.
Hurricanes blow away sickly sweet breadfruit and ripe papayas
and blow back disaster relief workers,
dry and withered from dying mainland cities.
Yet what is planted here, even briefly, must blossom.

Overshadowed by the sea, overshadowed by the land
Overshadowed by the lava rocks, overshadowed by the mountains
Overshadowed by the ruddy foreheads of the gods
I am living in a tent with seven tarot-reading social workers,
three anti-capitalist lesbians,
two psylocibin-soaked DeadHeads,
and a Cajun electrician from the Bayou.
It is the Cajun, I believe,
who roars all night like the ocean in my ear.
It is the Cajun who carries an extra jacket for me at all times.

Born were the fair-haired, they were strangers
Born were the peaked-heads, they were clumsy ones
Born were the messengers, they were sent here and there
Born were the disaster relief workers,
they were to fight non-stop amongst themselves.
And me, this timid *haole* girl who calls herself a journalist,
a peaked-head, a clumsy one,
one fairly objective messenger sent here and there
around the enemy camps.

Yes, meanwhile, these people pressed
six hours under mattresses
hurling prayers to the *aumakua*
and to Jesus and to *Pele*
and to every source of *mana*
they've been seasoned to respect.

Some who never open their windows
the pressure
their houses imploding into pick-up sticks around them.
An old man in boxer shorts six hours
trying to keep his possessions
from blowing into his neighbor's yard.
The roof does fly away, but just then
a peacock blows onto his lawn.
Now he's nursing it to health with dog food and *kukui* nuts.
He awaits the cold blessing of its 49 eyes.

The magenta *kumu*, the moray eel *puhi*,
the *uhu*, this indigo parrotfish
abandon the reef to splash their hot light in deeper waters.
They glide back in three days, now thick with the memory
of another kind of turbulence.
Before *Iniki* neighbors were nameless
they were hid and protected by dense green leaves.
Tonight they're asleep on the beach without guns.
Their dream bodies step over drunk *haole* construction workers
so their real bodies can trade food,
so their dream bodies can talk story.

Man for the narrow stream, woman for the broad stream
Seattle social workers near the vortex
colliding with surfer dudes from Orange County.
Here's the Cajun electrician discovering my secret—
he treats me precisely and consistently like a child.
I soften and regress with alarming speed;
now adolescent, now preverbal,

now just spiraling into some primal addiction,
a transfixed iridescent beetle on a too-short leash.
When the time comes to pry ourselves away from our lovers
we are not sure if the disaster was the hurricane or us.

The locals say,
"*Aloha*, you garish caricatures of quasi-spiritual pilgrims.
Later on, you sunstruck followers of the Grateful Dead."
"You can come back and clean up after the next tidal wave,"
they tell us, almost cheerfully.
"This island has a cataclysm approximately every ten years."

We go home to drive-by shootings in place of ponies
at birthday parties
and 2 A.M. emergency rooms with sticky vinyl seats.
In our minds we are gingerly lifting mushrooms out of cow patties.
We are wearing lurid tee-shirts
that say listen to the wind,
pay attention to its voice.

THE HAMPSTEAD HEATH KITE-FLYING FESTIVAL

All English children have rosy cheeks.
The ones who don't
are deported to France,
where gaunt faces
and huge, thoughtful eyes
are fashionable.
The children at the
Hampstead Heath Kite-Flying Festival
all had rosy cheeks
and tall, thin fathers with red beards
and wire-rimmed glasses;
fathers who held them on angular,
khaki-jacket shoulders to see the kites,
long, intellectual fingers
wrapped around tiny ankles.

Campbell McKellar and I at the
Hampstead Heath Kite-Flying Festival,
Campbell wearing his clear blue eyes
and his earnest chin,
I wearing my American citizenship like a scarlet letter.
Campbell went to school with Prince Charles,
who was flying his royal blue kite in Scotland that day.
Campbell McKellar and I with upturned faces,
looking at the kites.

Five hundred solid British citizens,
six months in the basement
making box kites out of peach and fuschia tissue paper
or making bird kites out of grey plastic bags
early, early mornings
in quiet little kitchens,
or ordering from catalogues:
"Chinese Dragon Kite Number 384:

Red, orange, green, and purple,
Seven feet long,
Watch it zig-zag through the air."

God loved the people at the
Hampstead Heath Kite-Flying Festival.
He sent them the only real spring day
I've ever seen in London.
There were hundreds of paper and plastic and plywood rainbows,
blue and violet and yellow angels
floating and drifting and diving and soaring;
weightless iridescent fish
dragging miles of fishing line up to heaven.

May all the kite flyers of Hampstead Heath
learn to make Tarzan kites;
kites with bulging biceps.
Holding invincible kite strings,
may they be lifted far beyond the sooty London air
to holidays on Venus and Neptune.
And may they all be back in time for tea.

BLESSING OF THE ANIMALS

"May all the beings in all the worlds be peaceful and happy."
—Vedantic prayer

She may have been overdressed
for Holy Saturday on Olvera Street,
adorned, as she was,
in tie-dye, pink roses, and white chiffon,
but at home she slept in a
flower-decked shrine to the Sacred Mother,
and this was one devout chihuahua
you would think was more than ready
for the Blessing of the Animals.
She expected, most likely,
a fine mist of Holy Water
sprinkling memories of heaven,
a vision held collectively
by the pig in the lavender frock,
the tortoises, parrots, ponies, chinchillas,
the goldfish in a jar held aloft by a watchful boy,
the ashes of dearly departed creatures
clutched in urns by Oaxacan widows,
and, most fervently of all, by one radiant cow,
leading all the diverse procession
with a yellow carnation cross
and a promise of resurrection.
Yet all good photographs are born in contrast,
which is why we are now iconic,
Getty Images of the blessing
for China, Utah, and points beyond.
Cardinal Mahony is generous with Holy Water.
Serenaded by Mariachis, we were baptized with a torrent.
The pious chihuahua, now cradled in my arms,
unintentionally flinched and braced against the soaking,
while I, furless, featherless,
water-blind in clip-on shades,
elated, rose to meet it like a wave.

PORTRAIT DE MADEMOISELLE RIVIÈRE

for Jean-Auguste-Dominique Ingres and his 1805 painting

Her neighbors say she's feigning Gothic.
She says, "Why should I live in my own century
when my own century is wrong?"
Mademoiselle Rivière was with her beloved
last night
and he loved her.
He loved her.
You can see it in her eyes.
Today, by the Seine,
she walks with her mother and aunt.
A young man stops to look at her.
She is radiant in her white dress
and he searches for an excuse
to walk in the same direction.
Mademoiselle Rivière does not notice.
She was with her beloved last night
and he loved her.
Mademoiselle Rivière's mother
smiles at everyone
when she walks with her idealized daughter
whose hair is sleeker than black jade,
whose skin can only be white velvet.
She is saying,
"Look quickly.
You may never see white velvet again."
Mademoiselle Rivière also smiles.
She is thinking of long, nectarian kisses.
She is absolutely certain he loves her.
You can see it in her eyes.
Soon they will stop at a café.
Mademoiselle Rivière will take off
her soft beige gloves
and play with the downy stole

draped around her like an amorous shadow.
While her mother and aunt are speaking,
she will remain
in luxurious silence.
Mademoiselle Rivière was with her beloved last night,
and he loved her.
For that moment, at least, he loved her.
You can see it in her eyes.

FALLING WEIGHTLESS

"Civil Unrest: Night Two"

West Coast lives don't drop like stones
or dense Newtonian apples.
They fall instead as milkweed,
posing weightless like horsetail or thistle;
now floating sun-baked
now blown to pieces
only here and there conscious
of a vague downward drift.

Curled up in a parking garage
a solid body becomes porous.
The Virgin of Guadalupe *is* on
the hood of that Chevy
but who can be sure about anything else?
Jim remembers flat bodies in flattened cars. . .
he's pulling them out with the jaws of life. . .
(at the station they call it the jaws of death)
and he's far from the only firefighter
in Calaveras County
to never stop drinking.

Do they take away your hose, we wonder
Do they take your reinforced polymer hat?
Jim becomes a forest ranger
and stares at one blue spruce
until it takes on the polished transparency of glass.
Still, his mind won't spiral inward
and such weeks are far too lonely.

Jim becomes an ornamental horticulturalist
and learns to raise calendula
and miniature pink roses.
But he remembers his daughter's eyes:

hazel,
an uneasy union of gold, green, and brown—
and he's drowning again,
falling like milkweed,
like thistle,
he's stumbling over the Candlestick Lilies
and African Violets

"I can't believe L.A. is burning," he says
"This is not a good time to be a homeless ex-firefighter."
The smell of smoke projects all the wrong slides:
small faces charred and stretched opalescent
fingers, forearms seared like young poultry. . .
But Jim's trained his brain to revisit a sex show in Saigon.
Delete days as an aide
at a psychiatric hospital.
He has learned to erase all the names
and the names
on those giant black slabs in D.C.

Jim stalks the Promenade in his thick red beard
less than ten minutes before curfew.
The streets are almost empty,
but he's trying to barter a Barbie doll for a drink.
The few beside him are mumbling about the benzene ring,
about old men deported to Holland,
about whether words like "curfew"
have an alternate definition
for people with no place to go.
Around them, fed by warm spring wind,
the fires will spread and roar till morning.

SOUTHERN LIGHTS

"Ever since Happiness heard your name
It has been running through the streets
Trying to find you."
          —Hafiz, interpreted by Daniel Ladinsky

I could swear I saw the Northern Lights
one night in Central Texas.
Ten thousand frogs and crickets
chanting and carrying on
about God knows what,
the sky switching on and off
with summer lightning . . .
stars so thick you could almost taste them,
surprisingly cool
and tart as lemon ice . . .
fireflies switching off and on, too,
almost in time with the summer lightning.
It's one of those Texas nights when
you feel all the parts of you open up and roll out easy
to distant points
in every possible direction.
It's one of those Texas nights
when you start to expect
the over-sized sky itself to open
and rain turquoise-eyed Tonkawa
with advanced degrees in anthropology.
This is when I can swear I see the Northern Lights in Texas,
and for at least five minutes,
even though I'm alone,
not one of the pillagers inside me is saying:
"My life wasn't supposed to turn out this way.
When did this happen?
How could this possibly have happened?"
referring to nothing in particular,
except perhaps the vague notion
of not being in the right place

at the right time.
Even a few days later
on the Fourth of July in Austin,
when 40,000 Texans and I
think it would be a good idea to see the Beach Boys
for three dollars apiece,
and it's still 94 dripping degrees at nine o'clock at night. . .
even when Omar and the Howlers
(as if we need a warm-up band)
howl seven unwelcome encores
of "You Can Call Me Rocky Cause I *Do* Know How to Rock,"
even then my spectral chorus of unhappy notions
is quieter than usual.
And later, when the Austin Junior Chamber of Commerce
gleefully announces
"The Biggest Fireworks Display Texas Has Ever Seen,"
and all 40,000 of us lie flat on our backs
to be personally ravished
by another facsimile of Aurora Borealis,
I really can't hear those malcontents at all.
Only the sound of the
Right Place
at the
Right Time
ricocheting off some low-rent section of the moon
and then landing quietly inside somewhere,
like the sound of a lover remembering to breathe.

Portuguese Bloodless Bullfight

"Every animal knows far more than you do."
—*Yellow Wolf, Nez Perce Indian*

Fiesta princesses in milk-white shorts
and cubic zirconium crowns
cradle red carnations and babies breath,
bending the August night with their lovely, provocative smiles.
The bull shifts slightly and practices assimilating
to this Southern California environment,
his pulse aligning rhythmically
with the pulse of a nearby car alarm,
inner ear already distinguishing
among shrill but subtle differences
in police, fire, and paramedic sirens.
For the Festival of the Holy Ghost
the *matador's* cape is hot pink instead of red.
His tights are chartreuse
and his suit of light, his *trajes de luces*
glitters new like the sun on a thousand blue lakes.
This means little to the bull, who like all bulls, is color-blind,
who has worked for the right to stand placid
and mildly lethargic
in this bloodless
and thoughtfully regulated new world.
Now the *picador* charges in again
to hurl his bright lance
at the soft, fleshy hump between the shoulderblades,
invoking the same law of physics
that governs laceless athletic shoes
and dull green examination gowns.
The bull bows to remind us
of the 613 articles of mercy,
and Velcro mates to Velcro with a sound all its own.

As one, the crowd tastes joy and wonder.
Men gulp red wine more viscous
than Robitussin
to toast both the *matador* and the bull,
because each will live to spread his seed
and neither will know his offspring.
A blessing is a blessing
And not to be taken lightly.

Keeping Conversation to a Minimum
on the San Francisco MUNI

She's rifling through the clear plastic bag
that holds her life on small pieces of paper,
meticulous writing in neat little rows
so that thoughts might line up
in neat little rows
like spices and herbs
in a carefully organized kitchen.
She serenades us all
with a fifties song:
It feels like heaven, being here with you,
Angel Baby, my Angel Baby. . .
fondling her hospital wristband,
now an I.D. bracelet from a sixth grade sweetheart.
When four thin young Gays from the Castro get on,
dead friends like rings on a tree
around their eyes,
she is the welcoming committee.
Now she's frantically happy,
even flirts with the gangstas when they get on.
The short one says,
"Show some respect Bitch,
or I'll knock you down on that sweet young ass."
It feels like heaven, being here with you.
Getting off the bus
she is burdened with choice.
Should she swing her hips like a girl,
swagger like an inmate,
or bop like a teenage boy?

We watch her alternate all three
through the lunch hour crowds
of Union Square,
as she mouths that song silent
like the words of the Rosary:
Angel Baby, my Angel Baby,
saving up all the sound
for a shield after dark.

IRISH UILLEAN PIPES

The piper has no lines on his palm;
only a surface smooth and polished as a skipping stone—
the kind you always looked for
because it resisted the water so little
that sometimes you'd get
four or five flawless arches in a row,
and whisper,
"Did I really do that or was it the stone?"

The piper with no lines on his palm
breathes his inner breath
in a country that lives in his heart but not in his blood.
They have music there that flows between joy and sorrow
like blue and orange heat in a flame.
He drinks the sorrow,
woven lengthwise into shadows
winding slowly around his solar plexus.
From the joy he forges bright transparent necklaces
to be placed by night
in the beak of a dark bird
who delivers them to drowning women
and abandoned saints.

The piper spends his off-days in a quiet room with no door.
You can get there by obsessing on
the relative merits of tradition vs. fusion
or the secret change in rhythm
that turned hipsters into beatniks.
You'll feel the subtle knitting of a wound.

Pilgrimage

You'll know it's time
when a bathroom mirror shatters,
sending tributaries of blood
down the length of your pale body.
The Great Mother whispers
"This is only who you think you are,"
but you're still busy
examining one slender stream of blood.
There it is—
it's trickling in a complicated pattern
from your right nipple.

You'll drive to the desert
through colors like prayers:
Manzanita, brittlebrush,
organ pipe cactus.
Three days later
eleven Piyutes in a pickup truck
find you lying face down on the dry red earth,
waiting for the Mother to grow roots from your palms.

You'll close your eyes a hundred times
on a hundred rocks
and still expect the Local Deity
to give you a different answer than love.

Again she chants only of mountains
trying to crumble to dust
trying to burst into flame
trying to drown in the sea.

Again she chants only of mountains
held together by love
for billions and billions of years.

Almost enough to hold together
your own small life,
fragile and strong
as the heart of a sparrow,
fragile and strong
as the heart of a red-winged hawk.

In the middle of the desert
you will fly over a lake.
The lake will give birth to an eagle.
In the middle of the desert
you will lose all capacity for discrimination.
Your only choice will be
to believe everyone
or believe no one.

Back home you will be like an urban coyote
howling at streetlamps
looking both ways before you cross the street.
Tasting the danger in everyday words,
tasting the kindness of danger,
your ears now prick up at slightly different angles
for each of the 17 colors of moonlight.

BLUE TRAIN RANT

You can tell all those people who go around singing
love train
peace train
people get ready there's a train a comin,'
you can tell all those people
if you can catch them between verses
that anyone who sees train as metaphor
for anything less shattering than Hydrogen Bomb
has never lived a block and three quarters
away from the railroad tracks.
They never slept close enough to hear that damn horn
blast three rows of nipples off a dog in heat,
blast six years of dust off a green velvet couch
and then blast them all back again,
now dirtier dust,
more irritable somehow.
There's a kind of religious optimism
you can only entertain in a semi-conscious state.
It happened just once,
it was four o'clock in the morning
and that drone,
it snuck up on me,
still far enough away
to be a pipe organ or even a harmonium,
one of those resonant instruments they use to call God.
Now this type of thing makes you think
maybe your life is about to turn around,
no maybe. . . maybe it already has.
But then it gets closer and closer and louder and louder
It blasts all the used tissues off of your bed
It blasts all wonder off the memory
of your first wet kiss,
leaving only the excess saliva behind.
It blows to pieces the second childhood

you were saving as a haven
for your last chilly days on a small, drafty planet.
And you think
this is the kind of spiritual experience I deserve;
this is an epiphany tailor-made for a person
who would smear Vaseline on the lens of her life,
who would shoot each experience in ultra-soft focus
air-brushing out any startling realities.
So this is what poetic justice is for:
that you should wind up living
not only a block and three quarters away from the railroad tracks,
but also directly across the street from the courthouse clock
that bangs out up to twelve bongs an hour,
precise as the pre-verbal hoof of Francis the Talking Mule,
and caddy corner from the Lutheran church
that chimes out
arbitrary hymns at arbitrary times
all week long, both day and night.
You get to hear *Avé Maria* sometimes,
but you also have to listen to *Bringing in the Sheaves*.
But it's the train, the train
that keeps you four feet to the left of your body.
And it's not like you never got moonstruck over a young Italian tourist
less than five minutes after Amtrakking out of the
San Diego station.
It's not like you never hopefully peered out the window
past that dusty depot in Albuquerque,
just in case your last long-haired, hang-gliding,
scuba-diving lover
might be leaving university to ride the rails awhile.
It's not like you're not aching in your bones
to roll away somewhere,
like you're not waiting for the curtains to blow open
and some strong-winged agent
swoops in like a bird of prey,
snatching you off to the land of endless freeways.
And if he's only happy with blood in his mouth,

fine, at least it will be your blood
this time, your deal.
It's not even that you didn't weep for joy
when the little engine that could
huffed and puffed all those toys
to the peak of glory mountain.
No, it's not the idea,
it's the X-rated decibels,
designed, perhaps, to scare cows off the tracks,
but serving, instead, only to make the deaf deafer.
Yes, now when that Motown bass starts playing
how long has that evening train been gone
you say not long enough, my friend,
not nearly long enough.

New Year's Eve Marathon, with Fireworks

The midnight runners are not afraid of falling into the sky—
this gleaming canopy of airborne sperm,
delirious, chasing its own pyrotechnic tail.
Midnight runners share an alternating current with
all frantic eruptions of aquamarine, indigo and scarlet;
emboldened, somehow, by scratchy recordings of *Auld Lang Syne,*
God Bless America, and even Frank Sinatra's *New York, New York.*
South to 59th Street,
northeast to 93rd,
8,000 together
are scrambling away from the year before
and the year before that,
afloat on this virgin splinter of time,
at once untouched by failure and
abandonment,
by progress-freezing patterns that halt all forces
but the ardent love of gravity for the aging human form...
The ones who don't stop for champagne at the halfway point
may actually burst through the barrier for all of us.
On Monday we will watch the news with hopeful eyes:
worldwide torture and disease mysteriously evaporated. . .
The Fox News talking head sneers when he reads
"It seems to have something to do with some
New Year's marathoner in a wombat suit,
surpassing the speed of worry in Central Park."
For us the trees at Tavern on the Green are spangled
with impossibly delicate lights
and the air, which smells vaguely of menstrual blood,
is fertile with unprecedented possibility.
The groom who carries his hyperventilating bride
across the finish line,
the nine who run together as one disjointed caterpillar,
the six-foot condom with a number on his chest
and a heart still strong in his windpipe. . .

They have mastered the five miles
without severely disabling injury
and will soon be followed by the majority
of their 7,988 friends.
The winner receives an athletic bag, a warm-up suit,
and a year free of nightmares
being chased by his own conversational errors.
The rest of us untie the sailor's knots in our exhales
and turn towards the future, and even the subway,
with something resembling courage,
and, at least for the moment, a sort of palpitating optimism.
In the morning the park will be littered with noisemakers
and a scattering of molted feathers
from a year well flown.

IV

THE
PATRON SAINT
OF
HIP

INSOMNIA

As a child,
not wanting to miss anything,
he refused to sleep for several weeks
until even grownups could clearly see
petite dream characters
scaling his torso with ropes and pulleys;
three carousing in his navel,
six cavorting on his collarbone,
seven sliding down his kneecaps
emitting crazed whoops of joy.
(Apparently this doesn't itch.)
Exhilarated by the boundaries
of our wakeful laws of physics,
how identity and place
are rarely morphed, dissolved, and switched,
they began to set down roots,
seek employment,
look for housing.
Inevitably, one night,
he couldn't help but fall asleep again.
The dreams never quite forgave him,
but now he knows what he isn't missing.

KNOWLEDGE

for my mother

I. My bird was yellow,
    bright as August sun.
    You let him perch on the frames
    of your never-finished paintings.
    Yellow wings soar near your ceiling;
    lemon streaks of motion.
    A yellow parakeet alights on your head
    while you sweep the floor,
    reminding you
    of golden light,
    flying around inside you once,
    perching behind your eyes.

II. Someone has been at the kitchen table,
    scribbling prayers on index cards.
    I spend hours,
    ear pressed against the gentle leaves
    of your garnet coleus,
    trying to hear what you hear.

Wapello, 1980

Hot summer nights in Wapello, Iowa
bored dogs yip and claw at screen doors
while eleventh graders cruise in wine-colored Buicks
and grey Ford pickups
up and down the same streets
over and over
catcalling to young blue-jeaned girls
who smile as they pass middle-aged farmers
who, now, without their John Deere caps,
are pink from the eyebrows down
and white from the eyebrows up.

Hot summer nights in Wapello, Iowa
folks had to drive fifty miles to see a movie.
Turn right at the EAT sign in front of Mae's diner,
go left at the green neon cross by the church.
Now straight and straight again
through empty cornfields,
steeped in promise.

See? Inside the darkened theatre
from each face, such robust light.

TRINITY SCHOOL: THE FINAL COUNTDOWN

Every morning at eight o'clock
Charles Bix floated onto that long yellow bus
radiant with new ways
to freak out the white girls.

In sixth grade
they thought they could still keep us out of trouble
with the famous boy/girl/boy/girl seating plan.
Guess they hadn't figured on Charles Bix
sidling up to the neighboring seats
left *and* right
to delicately hiss *"Do you wanna fuck?"*
in the middle of each documentary
about Brazilian exports
or even the manned space program.

In 1967,
nice girls were supposed to be easily shocked,
and I felt pretty bad
about not carrying my share of the burden.
But I *liked* things that rhymed,
better yet if bizarre and outrageous,
and it must have disappointed Charles Bix
when I asked him to sing
all his nastiest songs
over and over again.

Libby Kelly
ran crying to Miss Farinella,
this considered a more appropriate response.
Miss Farinella appeared genuinely appalled,
and I guess that attitude *worked* for her,
because that summer she married an Italian Count,
and flew off to live in a castle.

Before she was lifted away in his jet,
leaving the rest of us to lurch and pitch
into the lurid oil slick of junior high,
Miss Farinella told my mother I had a quiet beauty.
I spent the next 22 years
desperately trying to turn up the volume.
This had to be balanced with other important work,
like practicing magnificently demure expressions
every evening
in front of the mirror.

Charles Bix took advantage
of his miraculous smile
and that natural talent
for sexual harassment.
He went into either soft porn or politics;
nobody's sure which one.
Libby Kelly,
who can still blush better than anybody,
is day and night protected
by a tall, blue-eyed plumber
who excuses himself profusely
the rare times he swears
in her presence.

THE PATRON SAINT OF MELLOW

We're 13 years old,
we're smoking oregano,
we're listening to the egregiously laid back voice
of Alison S., the Night Bird,
and still nothing is happening.
We're ruining our Yogi Bear nightlights with these
eerie blue bulbs
greasy, dripping with patchouli oil,
and *still* nothing is happening.
Nobody ever said reinventing ourselves was going to be easy.

We're 13,
it's 1968,
we're learning, for the first time,
the hypocrisy of the acquired taste,
we're groovin' to Grand Funk Railroad
while our hearts are secretly crying low
for Chad and Jeremy,
we're forsaking the comforting, hyperactive A.M. patter
of Cousin Brucie and Murray the K
for that silver-eyed, black-feathered Night Bird
who apparently couldn't speak above a copacetic whisper
if she tried.

Alison S., The Night Bird,
who, with or without Quaaludes,
has a heartbeat slow and viscous
as that pulse dead deep in the center of the earth.
Alison S., of WNEW FM,
the acid rock station we leave on all night long
so it will be heard in the background
just in case somebody calls to gossip at 3 a.m.
"Just hangin' loose, Man
just listening to WNEW FM,"

Just practicing to get my voice
as mellow and unnatural
as that bogus, flippin' Night Bird,
the patron saint of hip.

First Day on the Job

The U.P.S. man saw a run in my stocking.
It was windy on the loading dock
and while it would be too much to say
my skirt billowed like a sail
or flapped like the wing of a seagull
or that anyone who saw it was even
remotely reminded
of Marilyn Monroe in "The Seven Year Itch,"
lemon silk sent swirling symmetrically
above her lovely young legs
by a sudden gust of air,
her child-like face flushed
and delighted
and confused;
the U.P.S. man *did* see a run in my stocking
when a breeze came and lifted
my beige cotton skirt just a little—
a run like a long white ladder
leaning against the house,
hiding behind a willow tree.
It seemed somehow dishonest
not to mention I had three more runs
hidden inside my boot.
The U.P.S. man smiled at me,
but I looked away because
I am not the new shipping clerk,
I am only a helper
or a woman
or someone foolish enough to wear a dress
when it's windy on the loading dock
and dust covers the office
like a fine layer of snow.

The Traveling Salesman and the Farmer's Daughter

The farmer's daughter's eyes are dark,
yet luminous as the moonlight.
The traveling salesman's a pusher of dreams.
He says, "Inside my bag are the stars and the sea.
Inside my bag are eleven gold rays
that could turn a poor girl to a princess."
The farmer's daughter says,
"My secrets hide. They sleep.
They are gifts for one who rustles through the trees
when the air is still as stone."
The farmer lies between sleep and waking
in his four-poster bed.
Everywhere, the cool, quiet evening whispers,
"That which is yours is yours forever."

Sleeping through Earth Day, 1970

Somewhere in Idaho
or Ohio
or Oklahoma;
somewhere in one of the O states,
there's a home for aging hippies
who are not even in love with love anymore.
He's there,
he's tired,
he doesn't remember me—
but every time he shakes his hips,
a tree grows in the rain forest.

When I was fifteen,
we thought everything we threw away
just disappeared forever.
Magic.
When I was fifteen,
tossing empty McDonald's cups out of blue convertibles,
my kindergarten teacher rolled down the window
of her Volkswagen Bug to yell at me.
She said, "You should be ashamed of yourself,"
and I was,
but not for that.
When I was fifteen,
my mother had been sitting on the edge of my bed
every morning
and every night
for as long as I could remember,
whispering "Love thy neighbor as thyself,"
the last thing before I closed my eyes
and the first thing before I opened them.
So there he was, the neighbor I was loving at the time,
he in his last year of high school
and me in my first,

he handing out Earth Day flyers in the hallway,
me busy dodging all those switchblades
in the girls' bathroom.

In 1970,
in the smoke-filled ghettos of New Rochelle High,
it was just two years since King fell
two years since another Kennedy fell
and there were at least 563 words
for the different colors of hate.
It wasn't enough to read *Soul on Ice*—
you could still get your cheek slit open with a razor blade,
you could still get trampled in the hall
between third and fourth period
by a stampede of rioters
too angry to care about Earth Day.
And the people who did know,
too busy trying to end the war
that followed the war
just after the war to end all wars;
and this the year they bombed Cambodia,
when every night before the 6:00 news
we had to send our hearts and minds out to play
or to pray
or at least to survive in one piece.
I was too numb to recognize Earth Day,
but *he* was watching.
When the New York sunsets learned new tricks,
washing over themselves with splash after splash
of six unearthly shades of self-illumined electric pink,
I cried for joy and he cried for
the ever-darkening air in our lungs.
He knew what "airborne particulate matter" meant even
and how our garish twilights were a joint venture
between the Divine Creator and the local industrialists.
Why the red tides were no longer the only days
when that sad smell came in from the ocean.
It came out in his music,

in those miracle arpeggios on the black and white keys,
in the notes he left on my desk in Biology,
goofy and soaring and surprisingly resonant.

And of course,
there were some things he *couldn't* understand,
like what I was saving
and who I was saving it for,
like why I wouldn't melt
into the glorious awkwardness
of our first explorations of desire
unless the Stones were singing *My Sweet Lady Jane*
over and over and over on the phonograph.
Like why I only knew how to love my neighbor
as I loved myself,
not nearly enough for either of us;
why after three months I stopped taking his calls
for no reason whatsoever.

Now, in yurts, in tie-dye longjohns,
at that home for aging hippies
they search for coded messages
in *Emerson Lake and Palmer* tunes,
grow their hair twice as long as before
to make up for the ever-spreading bald spot in the middle,
and somehow,
by adjusting the knobs on archaic guitars,
they are amping up the volume on our conscience.
One day, when Earth Day comes around again,
you notice
the small, perfect ears of your own child
and you're whispering
"Love thy *planet* as thyself."
One day you notice,
if you didn't forget to have children,
you're saying,
"Love thy planet as if everyone you've ever loved

would have no place to live if you didn't.
Love thy planet as if every river
carried strong red blood
for the veins of your beloved,
as if every empty field carried all the breath you would ever find
to fill the hollow spaces inside you."
You no longer throw paper cups out the window,
though now
you feel almost as guilty
when you haul them to the dumpster.

It doesn't matter how old you are,
your kindergarten teacher is always watching you,
your mother is always on the edge of your bed,
murmuring biblical injunctions you will not understand
for at least twenty years.
My friend,
my neighbor,
he hasn't really lost anything—
every time he flashes a grin,
a hole heals in the ozone layer.
Each time his hat stays on in the wind,
another tribe of untouchable indigenes
demand to speak their own language
and get it.
At least that's what I think
on the off days,
on the days when the things I've lost
seem immeasurably better
than the things I have.
Still, they tell us we're *supposed* to feel connected
to the moonrise
and the shadow of the moonrise,
to the silver-grey wolf
and the look in the eyes of the homeless.
We're supposed to feel connected
to Ecuador,

to Brazil,
to the rain forests of Rodondia,
where trees after trees,
that are taller and older
than prayers themselves
are disappearing right in the middle of the day.
How they're tilting the delicate balance
of the sun on our skin
and the sun on our soil.
We're supposed to feel connected
to El Salvador,
to Guatemala,
where *people* are disappearing
right in the middle of the night,
and whether or not we're alive enough to hear them,
they are tilting the delicate balance of our souls.

On Earth Day New Millenium we drive to the Eco-Fair
in luxury cars on luxury streets,
but no longer have the ghost
of the luxury of time.
We do have the luxury of the ground beneath our feet,
of all that is yet green and blue
and clay-colored around us.
We do have the heartbeat of the earth itself
still beating just loud enough
to sing us to sleep at night
and pray us awake in the morning,
so that thirty years later
we are still here,
we are still desperately trying to change,
and the sky is still open and willing to listen.

ACKNOWLEDGMENTS

G rateful acknowledgement is made to the following literary journals, magazines, and anthologies in which some of these poems were previously published: *Southern Poetry Review, G.W. Review, Americas Review, Hawai'i Review, Plazm, Sport Literate, Whelks Walk Review, Sanskrit, River Run, Curriculum Vitae, Poetry/L.A., Negative Capability, Aethlon, New Thought Journal, Magical Blend, Brownstone Review, Crosscurrents, Mind/Body Connection, Zuzu's Petals, The Synergist, Voices West, Explorations, Waterways, Sycamore Review, Mobius, Earth Bound, Dream International, Demitasse, Poetalk, Kinesis, The Denny Poems (anthology), Coffeehouse Poetry Anthology, 2000 Here's to Humanity (anthology), Collecting Moon Coins Anthology, Bubbeh Meisehs by Shayneh Maidelehs (anthology), Poetry Engagement Book (calendar), Marilyn, My Marilyn (anthology), Krax Magazine (England), Paris/ Atlantic (France), Takahe (New Zealand), The Dawn (Australia), Afterthoughts (Canada), Sivullinen (Finland), and others.*

ABOUT THE AUTHOR

Nancy Berg's poetry has been widely published in literary journals, anthologies, and magazines.*Oracles for Night Blooming Eccentrics* is a winner of the 2009 Blue Light Book Award. Nancy is also recipient of a Poetry Fellowship from the National Endowment for the Arts, a Whelks Walk Press Poetry Award, and a Pushcart Prize nomination, among other recognitions. She teaches with California Poets in the Schools and has an M.A. in Communication from Stanford University where she received a Fellowship on the basis of an original musical comedy screenplay. Raised by two cartoonists, Nancy began life as a cartoon, and later spent time as a lifeguard, a performer in a traveling tent show, a teacher of meditation, a university instructor, a disaster relief promoter, an evaluator of prognostications, and a small-time hula hoop savant, but she's primarily earned a living as a writer and editor in various media. Nancy Berg lives in Woodland Hills, California.

nancyberg@earthlink.net
nancyberg.com

Printed in The United States of America

www.ingramcontent.com/pod-product-compliance
Lightning Source LLC
Chambersburg PA
CBHW032017090426
42741CB00006B/632